Magnificent SAM

THE AMAZING ADVENTURES OF SAM HOUSTON

Written by Laurie Cockerell   Illustrated by Travis Dougherty

Laurie Cockerell

Kinderfable Press
Fort Worth, Texas

ISBN: 978-0-9845609-1-2
Library of Congress Control Number: 2012915865

Visit our website at www.magnificentsam.com

Publisher's Cataloging-In-Publication Data
(Prepared by The Donohue Group, Inc.)

Cockerell, Laurie.
    Magnificent Sam : the amazing adventures of Sam Houston / written by Laurie Cockerell ; illustrations
by Travis Dougherty.

    p. : ill. (some col.) ; cm.

    Interest age level: 005-014.
    Summary: Spans the life of Sam Houston from his childhood, to his years living with the Cherokee
Indians, to the early years of his political career in Tennessee, and finally to his move to Texas, where he
became the hero of the Texas Revolution, president of the Republic of Texas, U.S. senator and Texas
governor. Includes glossary, discussion questions, a timeline, and additional resources.
    Includes bibliographical references.
    ISBN-13: 978-0-9845609-1-2
    ISBN-10: 0-9845609-1-2

    1. Houston, Sam, 1793-1863--Juvenile literature. 2. Governors--Texas--Biography--Juvenile literature.
3. Governors--Tennessee--Biography--Juvenile literature. 4. Soldiers--Texas--Biography--Juvenile literature. 5. Houston, Sam, 1793-1863. 6. Governors--Texas. 7. Governors--Tennessee. 8. Soldiers--Texas.
9. Picture books. I. Dougherty, Travis. II. Title.

F390.H84 C63 2013
976.4/04/092   2012915865

Kinderfable Press
P.O. Box 10193
Fort Worth, Texas 76114-0193

Printed in the United States of America

T he old man spread a blanket under the shade of a giant oak tree.

Two children sat down to watch as Uncle Joe unfolded his pocket knife and began to whittle tiny bits of wood from the top of the nearly-finished cane.

The little girl gently ran her fingers over the cane's carvings. She traced a feather, a sword, a lone star....

"Uncle Joe, why did you carve the words *Magnificent Sam* here, along the side? Who is Sam? And what are all of these pictures about?"

The old man stopped his whittling and looked at the little girl. The twinkle in his eye could mean only one thing. He had a story to tell...and a good one.

"Scoot up here close, and I'll tell you the tale of a man like no other. He was a leader, a rabble-rouser, a peacemaker, a soldier, an adventurer, and one of the bravest men to ever walk this earth."

The old man adjusted his glasses and smiled.

"Some folks call him a rascal. Some folks call him a hero. But me? I just call him *Magnificent Sam*."

Little Sam was born March 2, 1793, in Virginia. That was long ago. The United States was a new country and George Washington was the president. The Houston family lived on a farm called Timber Ridge Plantation. Sam had eight brothers and sisters, and his daddy was a major in the army. Sam started going to school when he was eight years old, but he didn't like it much. What he did like was reading the exciting books he found in his father's library. Sam's favorite was a book about ancient Greek heroes called *The Iliad.*

Sadly, his father died when Sam was only thirteen. After that, his mama decided it was time to move to Tennessee, where they could begin fresh and live near relatives.

The day came for the family to leave the great plantation and the stately mansion that had been home to the Houstons for three generations. That morning Sam sat next to his mother, reins in his hand. Their two wagons were filled with bedding, furniture, tools, corn for the horses, dried fruit, flour, chickens, and the family Bible. And of course, they couldn't forget their guns, shot-pouches with well-filled powder horns, and plenty of newly molded bullets. Sam's mother carried his father's sword on her lap. Their neighbors waved as they watched the procession disappear into the forest—home of the bear, the wolf, and the Indians.

Several weeks later, the family settled near Maryville, Tennessee. The Houston brothers worked hard clearing the forest, building their log house, plowing the fields, and growing the corn. Sam's mother bought part of a general store, and some of his brothers worked there to help the family earn a living. But Sam didn't take to any of these chores. He still just wanted to read his beloved books. Sometimes, he disappeared into the woods and nobody knew where he was.

His mama was not too happy with Sam's aimlessness, and she eventually sent him to work in her store. Do you think he liked being confined in those walls, with no books to keep him company and no adventures to be had? No, sir. That sixteen-year-old boy craved excitement like the Greek heroes of old. He felt the call of the wild.

There was only one way to escape the broom and the plow.

Sam ran away into the woods. Ran across the Tennessee River to an island.

That boy ran away to live with the Indians!

Sam made friends with the Hiwassee Cherokee Indians who lived on that island. Since Sam's daddy was dead, Chief Oolooteka (some people called him John Jolly) adopted him as his very own and treated Sam like a son. Sam's new Indian father even gave him a special Indian name, Colonneh. That means "The Raven." A raven represented good luck to the tribe and would be a special symbol to Sam for the rest of his life.

Sam loved his new life. He could hunt, fish, listen to stories around the campfire, and play Indian games like lacrosse. Best of all, he could read his books whenever and wherever he wanted. Sam wore Indian clothes and grew his hair long like his Indian brothers.

One day his real brothers found him there on the island, reading a book, and begged him to come home. Sam refused. He told them he would rather measure deer tracks in the wild than calico cloth in the store.

He stayed with the Indians for three years. Every so often, Sam would go home to visit or buy clothes and gifts for his Indian friends. Since he didn't have a paying job, Sam had to buy on credit. Pretty soon he owed over one hundred dollars.

Sam may have been a runaway, but he was honest. He knew that a man must repay those he owes. He left his Indian family and returned home to Maryville, so that he could find a job and pay his bills.

Now, you will recollect that Sam did not like school when he was a young boy. It is quite surprising then, that Sam decided to become a teacher! He opened his very own school and charged eight dollars per student for a term's tuition. That was a lot of money in those days and more than any other teacher charged. Sam asked that his students split their tuition by paying one-third with cash, one-third with cotton cloth, and one-third with corn. Everyone was astonished when eighteen children and adults signed up to be students in his school.

The log schoolhouse had only one room. Sam could pull down the window shutters to let in light, but those shutters also served as desks. The students sat on wooden benches while Sam taught them all about history, geography, and Greek and Indian myths. When the weather was nice, everyone would take their lunch baskets outside and eat under the big oak tree that sheltered a spring of drinking water.

Sam was probably an interesting teacher, for he told many a grand tale about his adventures living with the Indians. Sam wore colorful calico shirts and still wore his hair in a long braid, just like an Indian. He whittled a sourwood stick with circular spirals, and carried it around the room as he spoke.

Sam made enough money to repay the debt he owed. His life as a teacher was satisfying and enjoyable, but the time had come for a daring and bold new adventure.

We all remember that the United States fought Great Britain to win its independence in the Revolutionary War. Less than forty years later, these two countries were at it again in the War of 1812.

Everyone was excited when American soldiers appeared in Maryville, donned in splendid pantaloons and waistcoats. They carried rifles, waved banners, and played the fife and drums. The army hoped to find volunteers to help fight the British again. One of the soldiers placed a handful of silver dollars on a drum. Everyone knew that if a man picked up one of the coins, it was his way of showing he wanted to join the army.

Our Magnificent Sam, twenty years old, picked up one of those silver dollars. Just like his daddy, he would be a soldier and fight the British. He would enter the army as a private. Some of his friends were surprised that he didn't want to be an officer like his father. Sam held his head high and said, "You don't know me now, but you shall hear of me."

Before he left, his mama gave him two very special things—his daddy's musket and a gold ring with the word *Honor* engraved inside. She told him how important it was to her that he be brave.

And so he was…brave as brave can be.

Soon after Sam joined the army, he met a very rugged and brave general named Andrew Jackson. In fact, people called him "Old Hickory," because they said he was as tough as hickory wood.

General Jackson was a very good leader and Sam was lucky to serve under him during the war. Their army was sent to Alabama to fight the Red Stick Creek Indians, after the warriors killed a large group of settlers at Fort Mims. General Jackson decided to attack the Red Sticks' fortification at Horseshoe Bend on the Tallapoosa River. The Indian camp was surrounded by the river on three sides. A big pine wood barrier protected the Indians, who were armed with bows and arrows, tomahawks, knives, and guns. Friendly Creek and Cherokee Indians helped General Jackson by quietly taking the enemy Creek canoes. Now Jackson's army could also approach the tribe's stronghold from the rear and cut off the Red Sticks' escape. Then, the attack began. An American soldier climbed over the log rampart and was killed. Our brave Sam followed that soldier, scaling the wall, his sword held high in his hand.

Suddenly, an arrow pierced Sam's leg! The arrow was barbed, and Sam could not pull it out. He asked another soldier to help him. The soldier pulled and pulled. He finally removed the arrow, but the wound was deep and bleeding. General Jackson ordered Sam out of the fray and to the surgeon.

The battle raged on. The General called for volunteers to storm the Creeks' new position. Up jumped Sam. Brave, brave Sam grabbed his musket and limped as he alone led the desperate charge. As he paused to rally his men and aim his gun, his arm and shoulder were struck by bullets. Sam fell. But the siege continued, and the Creeks were finally defeated.

The fort was taken. The battle was won. General Jackson got his victory.

And it looked like Sam was going to die.

But Sam was tough as nails. He didn't die. Those wounds that he suffered never completely healed, and they caused him problems for the rest of his life. Our Sam was now a hero. He was promoted to second lieutenant in the army, although the War of 1812 ended before he was well enough to return to battle. Yet Sam's adventures were far from over.

As more immigrants flocked to America and crowded into Tennessee, many of these settlers wanted to put down roots and homestead on the precious land where the Indians lived. So the government made a deal with the Cherokee Indians. The tribe was promised money and supplies if they would move across the Mississippi River. General Jackson remembered how Sam had once lived with the Hiwassee Indians, and offered him a job to help the tribe understand and abide by the treaty. Sam talked to his old friend Chief Oolooteka, and the Indians agreed to move.

Sam then led a group of Cherokee chiefs to meet and talk with President Monroe in Washington. Sam dressed in traditional Indian clothes during the visit, and Secretary of War Calhoun scolded him for wearing a "costume" instead of his military uniform. Shortly after that, a group of men tried to get Sam in trouble. They were angry because Sam had broken up a ring of slave smugglers. Although he was proven innocent, such a friend to the Indians would not abide this treatment. Sam resigned from the army in disgust, but continued to help the Cherokees as they prepared to move west.

Sam was now only twenty-five years old, but he had already been a teacher, a soldier, and an Indian agent. It seemed like Sam could do just about anything. And he could!

Sam decided to study law in Nashville. Most people studied and prepared for eighteen months before taking the test to become a lawyer, but Sam wasn't like most people. Sam was a quick study, and he passed the bar exam after only six months. He opened a law practice, and then became Nashville's Solicitor General (District Attorney) and major general of the Tennessee militia.

General Jackson had a big plantation home in Nashville called the Hermitage. He and Sam became good friends, and Sam visited often. General Jackson and his wife Rachel were like parents to Sam. They would remain friends for many, many years.

The General wanted to someday become president of the United States. He told Sam, "If you were in Congress, and if I were President, we could continue to work together and help our country grow."

With that goal in mind, Sam was elected to the U.S. House of Representatives!

Off went Congressman Sam Houston to Washington, D.C. Six weeks later, he was joined by General Jackson, the new U.S. Senator from Tennessee.

Perhaps those two good friends talked about an interesting area out west. A land of adventure, Indians, and lots of open space.

A land called Texas.

Sam represented Tennessee for four years in Washington. His friend Andrew Jackson still wanted to become the next president of the United States. If Sam was governor, he knew he could give his friend the kind of support he needed. So Sam Houston decided to run for Governor of Tennessee.

Sam enjoyed campaigning for governor. Can't you just imagine him wearing a satin vest over a bright Cherokee hunting shirt, a red sash, shoes with great big buckles, and a black beaver hat? The voters from Tennessee loved the tall, handsome man riding his stallion throughout the cities. They elected Sam as their Governor. He was only thirty-four years old.

Can you guess who became the next President of the United States?

That's right.

Andrew Jackson.

Once Sam became governor, he knew it was proper for a man in his position to have a wife. He married the beautiful Eliza Allen. We'll never know why, but soon after their wedding, Eliza decided to leave and move back to her family's home.

Sam was as sad as could be. He decided that he couldn't continue to be a good governor under the circumstances. So Sam resigned and decided to return to the people that gave him such happiness and peace. By now his Hiwassee tribe had moved to the banks of the Arkansas River in land that is today's Oklahoma. After a long trip, Sam stepped off the boat at Webber Falls. His adopted father Chief Oolooteka hugged Sam and held him tightly in his arms.

Returning to his Indian ways, Sam once again lived with the Cherokees and his adopted family. He wore Indian clothes and turkey feathers or turbans on his head. He even fell in love again with a young widow named Tiana Rogers. Sam decided to become a Cherokee citizen, so he and Tiana were married according to the customs of the tribe. They lived in a log house named Wigwam Neosho and opened a trading post there. Sam spoke the Indian language and did what he could to help his tribe.

Although Sam was happy to be back among his Indian family, he had days when he was very sad. It seemed there was still something missing in Sam's life. He wondered what it could be.

Sam loved his Indian friends and family. He did his best to help them, especially when they had to deal with the government. He made another special trip to Washington with a group of Cherokees. While he was there, a Congressman named William Stanbery accused Sam of fraud in dealings with the Indian tribes. Sam was a loyal and true friend to the Indians and he was mighty offended at this insult. The two men got into a scuffle, and Sam walloped Stanbery over his head and shoulders with his cane—right in the middle of the street! What a sight! They tussled and tumbled, and Stanbery tried to shoot Sam with his pistol. Fortunately, the gun misfired and Sam was not hurt.

Sam was arrested and put on trial. He hired a famous lawyer, Francis Scott Key (the man who wrote *The Star-Spangled Banner*). When Key became ill, Sam took over his own defense. He was such a fine speaker that the spectators filling the room cheered. Sam was still found guilty, but his punishment was only a mild reprimand.

After the trial, Sam visited with his old friend President Andrew Jackson. He told the President that the trial had actually, in a way, helped him. He felt like himself again… strong and ready for a new undertaking.

President Jackson talked again about that exciting land out west. The land was owned by Mexico and had, until recently, allowed the entry of new settlers from America. These settlers hoped that this land would become a separate Mexican state—or even a new republic. Together they decided that Sam could travel to Texas to promote a peace treaty with their Comanche Indians. He could also learn more about Texas and report back to the President.

Sam set his sights on a new adventure.

A new adventure in Texas.

Sam must have known that his new travels would take him away from his tribe and Wigwam Neosho for a very long time—maybe forever. Under the circumstances and by Cherokee custom, he gave Tiana their home and trading post so that she would have a place to live and be able to take care of herself. She would be free to marry another man someday, since Sam did not know if he would ever return.

Sam said good-bye to his Indian friends and his lovely Tiana. Astride his tailless pony Jack, Sam turned his face toward Texas. But before crossing the Red River, Sam traded Jack for another horse. He worried that a horse with no tail could not protect itself from the biting flies of Texas.

It was 1832 and Texas was still a part of Mexico. A man named Stephen F. Austin had helped many settlers move to Texas. But now, these settlers were unhappy with Mexico. They wanted the rights and freedoms that they expected and enjoyed in the United States. However, the Mexican government did not want to lose control of Texas, nor did they want the Texans to form their own laws and government.

During this time, a general named Antonio López de Santa Anna became president of Mexico and took full power of the country. He was a harsh dictator and the Texans became even more rebellious. When Mexican soldiers tried to take a cannon from the town of Gonzales, they found a flag with the words "COME AND TAKE IT." The cannon fired, and the Texas Revolution had begun.

Fortunately, it didn't take long for his fellow Texans to discover Sam's ability to lead. He was an important participant at meetings where decisions were made about separating from Mexico and beginning a new government. He was even chosen commander-in-chief of the Texas army.

Unfortunately, this did not mean much, and Sam was frustrated. He could not appoint his own officers, and the soldiers were not trained or prepared for battle. They needed guns. They needed supplies. They were not yet ready to fight the Mexican army.

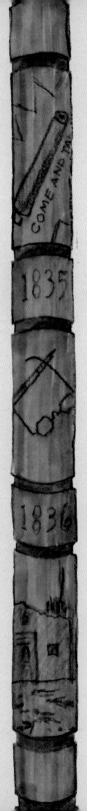

A small volunteer Texas army battled Mexican troops and gained control of San Antonio and the Alamo, an old Spanish church used as a military base. Sam knew that an even larger Mexican army would return soon, and the Alamo could not be defended against such an attack. He advised the officers to blow up and abandon the old stone building, but allowed Jim Bowie and others to use their best judgment. The men disagreed with Sam. They felt that San Antonio must and could be protected. They decided to stay and defend the Alamo.

Santa Anna and his army of over 2,000 soldiers arrived in San Antonio and demanded the surrender of the Alamo. Do you know how the Texans answered that demand? Colonel William B. Travis fired a cannon! The Texan army would stay and fight. Davy Crockett, Jim Bowie, Colonel Travis, and 186 other men took their battle positions. They vowed to never give up. Never surrender. Never retreat. They would fight to the death.

During this time, Sam and other Texas delegates met at Washington-on-the-Brazos to organize the new government. The weather was freezing, and the windows of the unfinished building where they met were covered only with cloth. Suddenly, a messenger arrived with terrible news from Colonel Travis. The Alamo was in trouble! Santa Anna's army was growing daily with reinforcements. The Texas army needed help!

Everyone was anxious to rescue their fellow Texans at the Alamo, but General Houston reminded them that they must first finish what they set out to do. They continued to discuss and write, and on March 2, 1836 (Sam's birthday), the Texans signed their Declaration of Independence. The Republic of Texas was born. The men elected leaders and wrote a new constitution. Sam vowed to gather soldiers and lead the troops to San Antonio, praying it would not be too late.

Sam left Washington-on-the-Brazos and headed towards San Antonio, rounding up volunteers and supplies along the way. When he stopped in the town of Gonzales, another messenger brought the worst news of all. For thirteen days, the 189 brave soldiers fought the relentless Mexican army. When Santa Anna's men climbed over the Alamo walls, all was lost. Every Texan soldier was killed.

Now every other Texan would remember.

They would never forget the Battle of the Alamo.

Santa Anna did not stop in San Antonio. He divided his army into three sections. He sent a portion of his army to Goliad, where Colonel James Fannin and his Texan soldiers were taken prisoner after the Battle of Coleto Creek. Santa Anna's cruelty continued when he sent orders to execute all the Texan prisoners. On Palm Sunday, 342 of these men were killed. Fortunately, some of the soldiers escaped to tell the story, and word of the massacre spread.

First, there was the Alamo. Now, there was Goliad. Texans wanted revenge.

Houston's army was still too small and needed more soldiers, weapons, and ammunition. He decided that the Texans were still no match for the Mexican army. Sam's army would march towards the east and the Sabine River. He hoped his plan would give the Texans time to prepare for the mighty battle to come. The newly elected Texas leaders told Sam to stop and fight Santa Anna's army, but Sam stood his ground and continued his march.

The Texas settlers were very frightened. Many people headed east for safety, joining Sam and his army as they plodded through the rain and mud. People call this retreat towards the Sabine River the "Runway Scrape." Families left almost everything behind as they scrambled to escape Santa Anna's army.

As the Mexican troops pursued the Texans, legend has it that Santa Anna sent a message. It said, "Mr. Houston, I know you're up there hiding in the bushes. As soon as I catch the other land thieves, I'm coming up there to smoke you out."

Sam was mad, but he was also smart. He sat in his tent, and thought while he whittled. He knew that his army must retreat until they were ready to stand and fight.

Sam planned and pondered and plotted.

MEXICAN ARMIES

TEXAS ARMY

TO NACOGDOCHES

Colorado R.

Brazos R.

San Jacinto

SAN JACINTO BATTLEGROUND

HARRISBURG

NEW WASHINGTON

Guadalupe R.

GONZALES

SAN ANTONIO de BEXAR

SAN FELIPE de AUSTIN

San Antonio R.

Navidad R.

Lavaca R.

GALVESTON

GOLIAD

VICTORIA

MATAGORDA

The RUNAWAY SCRAPE

Finally, Sam and his army came to a tree at a fork in the road. Its branches seemed to point south. Sam's army had become larger, better trained, and armed. Now, he decided, it was time to fight! The troops turned toward Harrisburg and Santa Anna's army. Both the Mexican and Texan armies set up camp near the San Jacinto River. General Houston stationed his army in the woods under a grove of oak trees.

That afternoon the Texan and Mexican armies exchanged cannon fire and a brief skirmish. Then…silence. Sam Houston slept that night with his saddle for a pillow. His soldiers were anxious to fight, but Sam learned many lessons from the Indians. He knew the importance of patience. He waited.

The sun rose the next morning, and Santa Anna felt confident. He knew he had many more soldiers than the Texan army. As the afternoon wore on with no gunfire, Santa Anna told his men to take an afternoon siesta. Sam sent some of his men to destroy Vince's Bridge, in order to slow the arrival of Mexican reinforcements and cut off escape for both Santa Anna's men and the Texas army.

While Santa Anna's army relaxed with their general asleep in his tent, Sam's army loaded the Twin Sister cannons (gifts from supporters in Ohio) and prepared for battle. They quietly mounted their horses and formed a long line. Sam jumped on a beautiful gray stallion named Saracen and raised his sword. When they were within firing range, the Texas army raced towards the Mexican camp shouting, "Remember the Alamo! Remember Goliad!"

Saracen was shot! Sam slid off his horse, landed on his feet, and mounted another horse. Soon Sam and his second horse were shot! The general's boot filled with blood, but still he would not leave the battle. Soldiers helped him onto a bay pony. The Texans continued to fight and Santa Anna's men could not move quickly enough. The Battle of San Jacinto was over in eighteen minutes, but the Texan army continued to take revenge and capture Mexican prisoners until dark.

Santa Anna was nowhere to be found. Texas was free. And Sam Houston was a hero.

The next day, two soldiers discovered Santa Anna hiding in tall grass. They marched the Mexican general to the Texan camp. Sam was resting under a large oak tree. Santa Anna blamed others and made excuses for the cruelties of the Alamo and Goliad. Many Texans wanted to see the dictator executed, but Sam knew Santa Anna was worth more alive than dead. Alive, the Mexican ruler could freely allow Texas to separate from Mexico in peace. Perhaps Texas could then claim independence without further bloodshed. On the other hand, if he were dead, Santa Anna would be just another soldier lying in the field.

Sam stood his ground again, and Santa Anna's life was spared. A few weeks later Santa Anna signed the Treaties of Velasco. He agreed to end the fighting, give back any Texas property taken by Mexico, and send Mexican troops home across the Rio Grande River.

Although both Sam Houston and Santa Anna led armies and countries, they were very different men. Santa Anna cancelled Mexico's constitution and took away freedom from his people. Sam Houston helped create a new constitution and fought to protect the freedom of his people. Santa Anna was dishonest and could not be trusted, even by his own country. And Sam? He could always be trusted to stand up and defend his beliefs. Sam didn't worry about the popularity of his decisions. He did what he thought was right and he stuck to his guns.

Sam lived up to the word inscribed inside his ring. *Honor*. Sam was a man of honor.

Texas was no longer a part of Mexico. It was now the Republic of Texas. The people of Texas recognized a good leader when they saw one, and they elected Sam as president of the new republic.

This was a time for new beginnings. Every country needs a flag, so the Texas flag with a gold lone star on a field of royal blue was born. The capital was moved from Columbia to a young town that was named after the Republic's first president, Houston. To save money, Sam's Presidential "mansion" was nothing but a log house with two rooms, where the floor was muddy and visitors sat on cots in the reception area.

It was also a time for rejoicing. On the first anniversary of the Battle of San Jacinto, a group of Indians surrounded the flagpole in the center of Houston. They danced in circles around the flag, honoring the new republic with their own ceremonial celebration. What a sight that must have been!

Even though the people were now free of Mexican rule, the new government had many issues to tackle. There were laws to be written, courts to be established, and debts to be paid. Sam continued to help the Indians and knew it was important for Texas to gain recognition from the United States and other countries. Sam worked hard. He hoped that someday Texas would become part of the United States. However, Sam's vice president, Mirabeau Lamar, did not like Sam and did not agree with his policies. Lamar did not want to see Texas annexed by the United States of America.

The Texas constitution only allowed the president to serve one term at a time, and Vice President Lamar was elected as the new president of the republic. Sam was upset when Lamar changed the flag (to the one we use today) and moved the capital from Houston to Austin. But he was truly furious when Lamar fought the Cherokee Indians, forcing the Texas tribes out into Oklahoma Indian Territory.

Lamar and Sam were very different people. They had very different plans for Texas. But Sam would return.

Sam was now free to travel and take care of personal business. While on a trip to Alabama, Sam met a beautiful young lady named Margaret Moffette Lea. She was twenty years old, with brown hair and violet eyes. The two fell in love and were soon engaged. After Sam was elected to serve as a representative in the Texas Congress, he and Margaret were married.

Margaret loved to write poetry, especially to her beloved Sam. She played the harp and guitar, and one of her favorite possessions was a rosewood piano. The Houstons took that piano with them every time they moved. They lived in several Texas towns, including Huntsville, Cedar Point, Independence, and Austin. Sam named two of their homes Raven Hill and Ravenmoor, just like the special name given to him by Chief Oolooteka.

Unfortunately, Margaret had many health problems and was unable to travel with Sam when he worked away from his family. She would stay home, caring for their children and tending her garden. Sam and Margaret were very much in love and missed each other terribly during those times. To make their time apart easier, they exchanged many long letters. Of course their most precious possessions were their eight children: Sam Jr., Nancy, Margaret, Mary, Antoinette, Andrew Jackson, William, and Temple.

Margaret knew that Sam had had struggles in his past. Sometimes he drank too much, but Margaret was very religious and had faith that Sam would be able to overcome this problem. With her help, Sam changed. He stopped drinking and started going to church.

The people of Texas remembered Sam's great leadership. When the time came to elect a new president of the republic, Sam was chosen to serve a second term. He moved the capital again, this time to Washington-on-the-Brazos.

Sam continued to promote the idea that Texas should join the United States. Some Americans thought that the addition of this large and beautiful land would make their country even stronger. However, it was the 1840s and trouble was brewing between the slave states in the south and the free states in the north. Texas allowed slavery during this time, and the northern states were worried that bringing another slave state into the union would tip the balance and give more power to the southern states.

Sam worked to improve relations with the Indians and pull Texas out of debt. Mirabeau Lamar spent five million dollars during his presidency, but Sam made very large budget cuts and spent only half a million dollars during his second term. Additionally, it seemed as though Santa Anna would never go away. His army still threatened the Texas border.

After Sam's second term as president ended, the United States decided to annex Texas. Sam was very happy that the dream he and Andrew Jackson shared would come true. Jackson had been like a father to Sam. They fought together in battle and worked together in Washington, D.C.

Sam received news that Jackson was very ill, and the Houston family traveled to the Hermitage to see him one last time. Unfortunately, Jackson died just a few hours before the Houstons arrived. Sam entered the room where Jackson lay. He held up two-year-old Sam Jr. and said, "My son, try to remember that you have looked upon the face of Andrew Jackson."

Sam put down his head and cried.

It would be reasonable to think that Sam would be ready to settle down now. He was fifty-three years old and had served as Tennessee governor and U.S. Representative, Texas Congressman, and President of Texas (twice!). But now that Texas was officially part of the United States, could there be anyone more perfect to represent the new 28th state in Washington, D.C.?

Along with his friend Thomas Rusk, Sam was off to Washington once again, this time as a U.S. senator. Soon Mexican soldiers attacked U.S. troops on the Texas border, and war broke out between the two countries. The Mexican-American War ended with the Treaty of Guadalupe Hidalgo and the transfer of a large section of Mexico's territory to the United States (land that is now all or part of New Mexico, Arizona, Colorado, Utah, Nevada, Wyoming, and California).

While Sam was far away in Washington, Margaret and the children stayed in Texas, patiently awaiting his next visit home. Senator Sam continued to whittle, wherever he was. He whittled during church, and he whittled with his feet on his desk. He would even whittle toys for children.

Of course, Sam didn't dress like the other senators. He would sometimes wear a Mexican blanket and a sombrero. He particularly loved to wear his leopard skin vest. He told people that he wore it because the Bible says that a leopard cannot change its spots. That was Sam. He stuck to his guns. He was an individual and didn't change his beliefs or behavior to please other people. He stood up for what he believed was right.

Margaret always hoped that Sam would share her faith, and was happy and relieved when Sam decided to join the church. While on a trip home to Texas, Sam was baptized in the chilly waters of Rocky Creek. Friends and family looked on and smiled, and Margaret gave a little shout of joy. After the baptism, one of his friends said, "General, I hear your sins have been washed away." Sam replied, "I hope so. But if they were all washed away, the Lord help the fish down below!"

Senator Sam gave many speeches in Washington. He was worried because some states considered leaving the United States over the issue of slavery. If those Southern states decided to secede, Sam knew that civil war was likely. He also knew that the North would probably win.

It was a very confusing time. Sam had fought hard to see Texas join the United States and fought hard to keep it there. He did not want to see his beloved state leave the Union.

America needed a strong leader during those days. Some people thought Sam would make a good president. They believed he could help keep the United States together and maybe even prevent a war. He was a man who understood both the importance of states' rights and the need to protect the Union.

However, Sam was almost sixty-six years old and had been a senator for thirteen years. He decided to retire from Washington and return home. He knew that Texas was thinking about secession and he believed he could protect his state if he were governor. The state's citizens agreed, and Sam became the seventh governor of Texas.

The Houstons moved into the governor's mansion in Austin, which was now the state's permanent capital. This mansion was very different from the log cabin Sam lived in when he was president!

The Houston children enjoyed having their Daddy home and living in such a big house. When Sam's son Andrew Jackson Houston was five years old, he locked a group of senators in a room in the capitol building. He hid the key in a flower bed and then refused to unlock the door. Finally, Governor Sam told Andrew that he must find the key and unlock the door or Andrew would be locked up too…in jail!

Andrew brought the key to his father and the senators were set free.

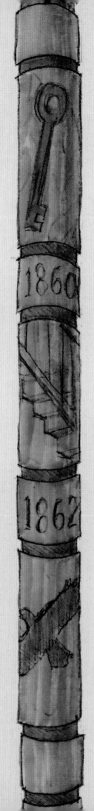

Abraham Lincoln became president in 1860 and the southern states almost immediately began to secede. They believed that states should have the final decision on issues like slavery. They formed their own country called the Confederate States of America.

Even though Sam believed that states had the right to make most of their own decisions, he did not want to see Texas leave the United States. However, many Texans wanted to join this Confederacy, and the people soon voted to secede.

Everyone in the Texas government was now required to swear an oath of loyalty to the Confederacy. Would Sam sign that promise? Would a leopard change its spots?

He did not. Sam refused to pledge loyalty to the Confederacy. A new temporary governor was appointed, and the Houstons were told that they must leave the Governor's mansion. The family packed their bags and moved back to their home in Cedar Point near Galveston Bay.

Two weeks later, the Civil War began. When Union gunboats entered Galveston Harbor, the Houstons moved to Huntsville. They found a very interesting house that was shaped like a steamboat.

It was on the front porch of this house that Sam called his servants with important news. He read aloud Lincoln's *Emancipation Proclamation*, then announced that he would now free all of his slaves. For a moment there was silence. His servants didn't know whether to jump for joy or cry. Sam had always been kind and generous to those who worked for him. He made sure that his slaves were educated and allowed them to hold outside jobs and keep their earnings. Some of his slaves feared that they would be forced to leave the Houston home. They were happy to hear that Sam would let them continue to work and care for his family as paid servants.

As time passed, Sam liked to sit under the big, shady oak tree in his yard. Indian friends came by to visit.

Sam thought about his life.

He thought about his childhood in Virginia...how he loved to read, more than he loved to go to school.

He remembered his years living with the Indians in Tennessee...the lessons they taught him...the friendships he made.

He thought about his military battles and adventures...Horseshoe Bend, San Jacinto...and the ring his mother gave him with the word *Honor* inscribed inside the gold band.

He thought about his political career...U.S. Representative and Governor of Tennessee, Indian Agent, Texas President, Texas Congressman, U.S. Senator, and Texas Governor.

He thought about his family...his son Sam, who fought for the South and was injured in the Civil War, but survived—maybe because the small Bible Margaret gave him diverted the bullet's path...his daughter Nannie, who was so much like her father... and mischievous little Andrew.

He thought about his good friend Andrew Jackson...so many of their dreams and plans had come true.

When Sam was seventy years old, he became very ill. As he lay dying, surrounded by his loving family, we know his final thoughts. For he said,

"Texas! Texas! Margaret."

Texas Texas Margaret

"And that, my children, is the story of Sam Houston. He was honest, brave, and strong. He loved the United States, and he loved his Texas."

Uncle Joe gently blew the wood shavings off the side of the cane. The children leaned in and peered at the final carving. They smiled, and Uncle Joe winked and nodded his head.

"Yep, he was magnificent all right," said the old man.

"*Magnificent Sam.*"

GLOSSARY

annex: To add to something larger; in this case, to add Texas as a state to the United States

calico: A course cotton cloth, usually printed with bright designs

Confederacy: The eleven Southern states that seceded from the United States during the Civil War

delegate: A person who acts as a representative for others, usually at a meeting or conference

dictator: A ruler (usually oppressive) that has supreme authority over a country and government

Emancipation Proclamation: President Lincoln's executive order issued during the Civil War, proclaiming freedom for slaves who lived in those territories that were rebelling against the federal government

immigrants: People who move from one country to permanently settle in another country

Indian: The term Indian used in this book refers to the group of people and tribes now more commonly referred to as Native Americans; *Indian* was the term normally used during Sam's lifetime

massacre: The unnecessary and savage killing of a large number of people

militia: A citizen army (not professional soldiers)

musket: A long-barreled shoulder gun, usually used by the infantry

pantaloons: Men's tight pants that extended from the hip to the ankle

plantation: A large estate or farm where crops are grown

powder horn: A container made from an animal's horn, used to carry gunpowder

reprimand: To criticize sharply or scold

republic: A form of government where the leader is not a king (often the leader is a president); the supreme power of a republic is held by the people and their elected representatives

secede: To withdraw membership from an organization; in this case, states withdrew from the Union

siesta: A rest or nap, usually taken after a midday meal

skirmish: A small battle during a war or larger conflict

sombrero: A broad-brimmed Mexican hat

steamboat: A ship powered by steam, often equipped with paddlewheels

Union: The United States of America—during the Civil War, the northern states were often referred to as the Union; the southern states, the Confederacy

waistcoat: A vest

DISCUSSION QUESTIONS

1. Sam Houston was greatly influenced by books, people, and experiences in his life. Discuss how Andrew Jackson, Chief Oolooteka, Sam's teaching experience, and the ring given to him by his mother may have affected future decisions made by Sam.

2. Sam's *Honor* ring reflected one of his most endearing character traits. Design a ring that reflects your personality and goals.

3. Historical events guide the future of a country and the lives of its citizens. What if…
   (1) Stanbery's gun had not misfired, (2) Sam had not resigned as Tennessee governor, (3) Sam's army had not retreated during the Runway Scrape, (4) the Texan army had lost the Battle of San Jacinto, and (5) Sam had been elected president of the United States?

4. Imagine that you are the president of a new republic. What would you name your country? Design a flag and write a constitution that would be the foundation of your new country's principles.

5. Pick your favorite Texas hero. Paint a portrait of him (or her!) and list five major accomplishments.

6. Most Texans hoped that Texas would be annexed and become part of the United States, but there were some who preferred to remain a separate country. Find a partner and debate the pros and cons of a republic versus annexation to the United States.

7. Pretend that your family is moving in a wagon train during the 1800s. Make a packing list, then draw a picture of the inside of your wagon and the supplies you would bring.

8. Write descriptions and draw pictures of the Battle of San Jacinto from both Sam Houston's and Santa Anna's perspectives. Then find and read Sam's and Santa Anna's actual accounts of the battle.

9. Look at a Texas map and find the location of the following places and events: The Alamo (San Antonio), The Battle of San Jacinto, Goliad, Gonzales, Austin, Houston, Columbia, Nacogdoches, and the Texas Declaration of Independence (Washington-on-the-Brazos).

10. Sam struggled with difficult decisions after Texas decided to secede from the Union. Put yourself in Sam's shoes. Make a list of the benefits and risks associated with seceding, joining the Confederacy, or remaining as a state of the Union. What would you do?

TIMELINE

1793   Sam is born March 2 in Rockbridge County, Virginia

1807   Sam's family moves to a farm near Maryville, Tennessee (13 YRS OLD)

1809   Sam runs away to live with the Cherokee Indians on Hiwassee Island (16 YRS OLD)

1812   Sam teaches school near Maryville, Tennessee (19 YRS OLD)

1813   Sam enlists in the army (20 YRS OLD)

1814   Sam injured at the Battle of Horseshoe Bend (21 YRS OLD)

1817   Sam becomes an Indian sub-agent (24 YRS OLD)

1818   Sam studies and becomes a lawyer (25 YRS OLD)

1823   Sam represents Tennessee in U.S. House of Representatives (1823-27) (30 YRS OLD)

1827   Sam elected governor of Tennessee (1827-29) (34 YRS OLD)

1829   Sam marries Eliza Allen in Tennessee (35 YRS OLD)

           *they separate and Sam resigns and moves to live again with the Hiwassee Cherokees (who had since moved to present-day Oklahoma)

1832   Sam has confrontation with Congressman Stanbery in Washington (39 YRS OLD)

           *Sam travels to Texas

1833   Sam elected delegate to the Convention of 1833 in San Felipe (40 YRS OLD)

           *Santa Anna becomes president of Mexico

1835   Battle of Gonzales and Texas Revolution begins (42 YRS OLD)

           *Sam serves as delegate to San Felipe Consultation

           *Sam named Major General of the Texas army

1836	Texas Declaration of Independence is signed and new constitution written at convention at Washington-on-the-Brazos (43 YRS OLD)

1836 Texas Declaration of Independence is signed and new constitution written at convention at Washington-on-the-Brazos (43 YRS OLD)
      *Sam confirmed Commander in Chief of the army
      *The siege of the Alamo
      *The Runaway Scrape
      *The Battle of San Jacinto
      *Sam elected President of the Republic of Texas (1836-38)

1839 Sam elected to represent San Augustine in the Texas Congress (46 YRS OLD)

1840 Sam marries Margaret Lea in Marion, Alabama (47 YRS OLD)
      *Sam reelected to serve second term in Texas Congress

1841 Sam elected to second term as President of Republic of Texas (1841-44) (48 YRS OLD)

1845 Texas annexed and admitted as the 28th state to the Union (52 YRS OLD)

1846 Sam represents Texas in the United States Senate (1846-1859) (53 YRS OLD)
      *Mexican-American War begins

1854 Sam baptized in Rocky Creek (61 YRS OLD)

1859 Sam elected governor of Texas (1859-1861) (66 YRS OLD)

1861 Texas secedes from the Union (68 YRS OLD)
      *Sam refuses to sign pledge of loyalty to the Confederacy and is forced to step down as Governor
      *The Civil War begins

1863 Sam dies at the Steamboat House in Huntsville, Texas (70 YRS OLD)

RESOURCES

BOOKS

SAM HOUSTON, by James L. Haley. Norman, Oklahoma: The University of Oklahoma Press, 2002.

SAM HOUSTON: FOR TEXAS AND THE UNION, by Walter M. Woodward. New York, New York: The Rosen Publishing Group, Inc, 2003.

EIGHTEEN MINUTES: THE BATTLE OF SAN JACINTO, by Stephen L. Moore. Maryland: The Rowman & Littlefield Publishing Group, Inc., 2004.

THE RAVEN, by Marquis James. New York: Blue Ribbon Books, 1936.

MAKE WAY FOR SAM HOUSTON, by Jean Fritz. New York: Putnam and Grosset Group, 1986.

SAM HOUSTON AND THE AMERICAN SOUTHWEST, by Randolph Campbell. New York: Pearson Longman, 2007.

WEBSITES

www.magnificentsam.com ...*information about "Magnificent Sam", resources, and links*

www.samhoustonmovie.com ...*numerous resources, videos, and links*

www.thealamo.org ...*resources and information about the Alamo*

www.samhoustonhistoricschoolhouse.org ...*information about Sam's school in Tennessee*

www.nps.gov/hobe ...*learn more about the Battle of Horseshoe Bend in Alabama*

www.thc.state.tx.us ...*Texas Historical Commission's site*

www.sanjacinto-museum.org ...*learn all about the Battle of San Jacinto, the current site, and the museum*

www.nmai.si.edu ...*learn about Native American histories and cultures*

www.birthplaceoftexas.com and www.txindependence.org ...*interactive tools and information about the history of Washington-on-the-Brazos and the Texas Revolution*

www.thehermitage.com ...*history of the Hermitage and Andrew Jackson*

If you would like to learn more, you will find many interesting and useful websites using the search words **Sam Houston, Texas Revolution,** *and* **Texas history.**

MOVIES

SAM HOUSTON: AMERICAN STATESMAN, SOLDIER, AND PIONEER [DVD]. Florian, D. (Producer). 2011.
Available from www.samhoustonmovie.com
THE ALAMO [DVD]. United States: Touchstone Pictures. 2004.
GONE TO TEXAS [DVD]. United States: Republic Pictures. 2001.

PLACES TO VISIT

TENNESSEE
The Sam Houston Schoolhouse (Maryville)
Sam Houston home site (Maryville)
Cades Cove-Thompson Brown House (Maryville)
The Hermitage (Nashville)

ALABAMA
Horseshoe Bend National Military Park

TEXAS
The Alamo (San Antonio)
Independence Hall and Star of the Republic
Museum (Washington, Texas)
Fannin Battleground (Goliad)
Sam Houston Memorial Museum, Steamboat and Woodland Homes,
Sam Houston Tomb/Gravesite, Sam Houston Statue (Huntsville)
Independence Baptist Church, Sam's baptism site on Rocky Creek,
site of Houston home and Margaret's 1863 home, gravesites
of Margaret, Nancy Lea, and Eliza (Independence)
San Jacinto Monument/Battleground/Museum (LaPorte)
San Felipe de Austin State Historic Site (San Felipe)
Texas State Capitol and governor's mansion (Austin)

Photos (clockwise): Steamboat House, Sam Houston Schoolhouse,
Sam Houston statue, the Alamo, San Jacinto Monument, Independence Hall

ACKNOWLEDGMENTS

First and foremost, we must give thanks and credit to our Great-Uncle Joseph McCallie. In 1939, "Uncle Joe" gave a speech to the Daughters of the War of 1812 about the life of Sam Houston, the grandson of his great-great grandmother's brother. The script was uncovered during our mother's genealogy quest, and was the inspiration for *Magnificent Sam*.

Special thanks to Denton Florian and Mayor Mac Woodward for sharing their expertise and knowledge, and author James Haley, whose biography of Sam Houston provided such a rich foundation of information. Thanks also to the following for their generous assistance with attention to historical detail both in illustration and story text: Sherri Driscoll (the Alamo), Stephen L. Moore (San Jacinto), Bob and Mary Lynne Bell (Historic Sam Houston Schoolhouse), Ove Jenson (Horseshoe Bend), James Yasko and Marsha Mullin (the Hermitage), Gloria Motter (Cades-Cove Thompson Brown House Museum), Pauline Morrissey (Maryville), and Charlie Fogarty (Texas history).

Yvonne Cumberland provided unparalleled editing assistance and Texas history education expertise. Many thanks also to our dear friend, Dr. Carolyn Rude, as well as others who participated in the editing process: Terri Stuenkel, Georgann Muckleroy, Jameson Cockerell, and of course our most beloved editors—Mom and Dad.

Thanks also to our technical heroes: Daron Cockerell (book design assistance), Craig Landers (Taylor Specialty Books), Harry Gendel (home base for illustrating), Bailey, Ryder, Dylan, Mike, Tami, and Mimi (models), and Simon Powney (rendering expertise). Their knowledge, skill, and patience are greatly appreciated.

Of course, this project would have never been completed without our wonderful families. Special thanks to Sharie, Bailey, and Ryder for their patience with marker stains on the tablecloth, as well as the endless household disruptions that come with a two-year book creation project. Thanks also to Jesse, Molly, David, Ben, and Kyle for their advice and patient endurance with many visits to the library, Texas history dinner table discussions and movies, trips across the country to historic sites, and shelves covered in every Sam Houston book ever written.

And finally, thanks to General Houston and the real-life cast of characters who brought courage and honor to their Texas, their families, and their country. And to Margaret…whose magnificent faith and love for her husband shaped twenty-three grand and glorious years in the life of one of our country's most significant heroes.

A BRAVE SOLDIER.
A FEARLESS STATESMAN.

A GREAT ORATOR -
A PURE PATRIOT.

A FAITHFUL FRIEND,
A LOYAL CITIZEN.

A DEVOTED HUSBAND
AND FATHER.

A CONSISTENT CHRISTIAN -
AN HONEST MAN.

Inscription on
General Sam Houston's Tomb
Huntsville, Texas

ILLUSTRATIONS AND PHOTOGRAPHS

Photographs:

The image of General Houston seen on the book cover is based on the original photograph (**see acknowledgments, page 63**) by Charles DeForest Fredricks of New York City (circa 1857), courtesy of Sam Houston Memorial Museum, Huntsville, Texas.
The Alamo photograph (**see resources, page 61**) is provided courtesy of photographer Grace Mercado-Marx.

Illustrations:

Page 4: It seemed appropriate that Uncle Joe would tell the story of Magnificent Sam under the famous Sam Houston Oak (also known as the Runaway Scrape Oak), found near Gonzales, Texas on the property near the historic McClure-Braches home. It is said to be the site where General Houston and his army camped after the burning of Gonzales and the beginning of the Runaway Scrape.

1812: You can still visit the Sam Houston Schoolhouse in Maryville, Tennessee. You can walk around inside the schoolhouse, and find many other interesting artifacts within the nearby museum.

1818-23: The Hermitage today looks very different from the Hermitage seen in the background of this picture (set in the 1820s). This earlier version was remodeled in 1831 and again in 1837 (after a fire in 1834).

1823-27: The building you see in this picture is modeled after a home in Maryville, Tennessee that now houses the Cades Cove-Thompson Brown House museum. Although Sam may not have campaigned in front of this particular building, this home (a two pen dog trot) was built prior to 1798, so would have been in existence during the time of Sam's campaign for governor. You can still visit this building, now a museum run by the Cades Cove Preservation Association.

1836: You can find several renditions of this particular surrender scene (the illustration in this book is inspired by William Henry Huddle's 1886 painting, *The Surrender of Santa Anna*), but most of these paintings show General Houston's right leg bandaged. However, in an 1853 letter to Margaret, Sam writes, "I suffer slightly in my left leg, from the same cause, that I complained of at home, the San Jacinto wound." (See *The Personal Correspondence of Sam Houston*, edited by his great-great granddaughter, Madge Thornall Roberts).

1836-41: Look at the house directly behind the flagpole and to the left. This home replicates the "executive mansion" that belonged to President Sam Houston of the Republic of Texas. He lived in a small log house, very different from today's White House or the governor's mansion where the Houston family lived in later years. The famous naturalist John James Audubon visited the cabin, noting that it had only two rooms, a large burning fire, campbeds, and muddy floors. The home was located in the area that is now downtown Houston.

1846-54: The leopard skin vest and the beautiful Mexican blanket in this picture represent Sam's lifelong appreciation of colorful and symbolic fashions from a variety of cultures.

1859: That is the Texas Capitol that you see in the background behind Andrew Jackson Houston. But if you visit Austin today, you will see a different pink granite building. The structure seen in this illustration burned in 1881, and the new building was completed in 1888.

1863: From *The Iliad* of his childhood to the final moments of his life with his family by his side, enjoy walking through this quilt-like journey of the amazing adventures of *Magnificent Sam*.